A glass jar.
A medicine bottle.
A pencil.
A ruler.
A tennis ball.
An empty tin.
Plasticine—a few pieces.
A coin.
A comb.
A reel of sticky tape.
Some toy soldiers.
Some water colours.
Two cardboard boxes.
An empty cotton reel.

Series 621

Did you know that white light is made up of all the colours of the rainbow?

With simple instructions and wonderful coloured illustrations, this fascinating Ladybird Junior Science Book not only shows you how easily this can be proved, but also explains how light can be bent (to see round corners), reflected, used to magnify, to cast shadows or project an image on the wall, how essential light is to life, and how your own eyes work.

All the materials used for the experiments and models are simple, safe and easily obtainable.

The Publishers wish to acknowledge the helpful interest and encouragement given by J. Cottam, Dip.Ed. (Headmaster) *in the early stages of planning this series.*

A Ladybird Junior Science Book

LIGHT, MIRRORS and LENSES

by F. E. NEWING, B.Sc.
and RICHARD BOWOOD

with illustrations by
J. H. WINGFIELD

Publishers: Wills & Hepworth Ltd., Loughborough

First published 1962   ©   *Printed in England*

Light and Darkness

The children in the picture went into a room in the early morning. They knew there was a bowl of apples on the table, but even though their eyes were wide open they could not see them *because it was dark*.

Think about that for a moment. Dark means *no light*. When we go into a room and say that it is dark, what we really mean is that no light is reaching us from anything in that room. Without light coming from something to our eyes we cannot see it. We only see when light enters our eyes.

The girl drew the curtains a little and light came into the room. Some light which fell on the apples was scattered throughout the room, and reached the children's eyes. Then they could see the apples.

We say that cats can see in the dark. That is not really true. The fact is that cats, and other animals which hunt at night, can see better than we can in a poor light. If it is absolutely dark, with no light at all, even cats cannot see.

In this book we are going to find out something about light, by doing experiments and making models. We shall find out how light behaves when it strikes mirrors and lenses, and how we make use of its properties. But even the scientist does not yet fully understand exactly what light is.

4

Eyes

Look carefully at your eyes in a mirror. You will see a coloured circle, blue, brown or grey, in the white eye-ball. The coloured circle is the *iris*, and the small black circle in the iris is the *pupil*. The pupil is really an opening, which looks black because the inside of the eye is dark.

You *see* when light goes through the pupil and falls on the special screen at the back of the eye, called the *retina*. A picture of what you are looking at is formed on the retina.

You can get some idea of how an eye works with a model. You need a glass bowl, such as a goldfish bowl, full of water. Make a small hole in a piece of cardboard to represent the pupil of the eye. Stand a lighted candle a short distance from it. Switch off the light or draw the curtains, to darken the room. Now hold a piece of white paper behind the bowl, on the opposite side to the candle. This represents the retina. Move the paper about until you see the candle on it.

The candle will appear smaller and upside down. This is called the *image* of the candle. If we made a perfect model the piece of white paper would be stuck on to the side of the bowl, which represents the eyeball.

The retina is very sensitive, and can be damaged by too much light. That is why 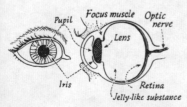 you must never look directly at the bright sun with the naked eye. Watch your eye in a mirror when you shine a torch into it for a second or two. The pupil will close automatically to protect the retina.

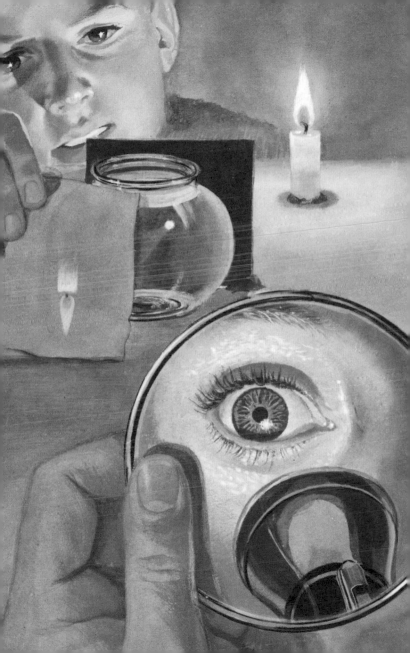

Shadows

We have found that darkness is where there is no light. When something stops light falling on a surface, it forms a shadow. A small naked torch bulb casts a sharp shadow because all the light comes from one place. A shaded light casts a shadow with fuzzy edges because the light comes from all over the shade.

We all know how to make animal shadows with our hands held between a bright light and a wall. You will find that the shadow is biggest when your hands are close to the light, and it is sharpest when the shadow is made by a small bright light.

Sometimes we can see the shadow of the earth cast on the moon, which is about 240,000 miles away. This is called an eclipse of the moon. We see the moon because light from the sun is falling on it, and an eclipse of the moon occurs when the earth happens to come between the moon and the sun, and stops the light from the sun reaching the moon.

If the moon comes between the sun and the earth it may cast its shadow on the earth's surface. If you happen to be in that shadow you will see an eclipse of the sun, as the moon passes across the sun's face.

Not all shadows are black and grey. You can make coloured shadows. Cover the fronts of two torches with different coloured cellophane, such as red and blue sweet-wrappings. Stand a small object in front of a sheet of white paper and shine the torches on to it. You will see two coloured shadows and a different coloured background. Repeat the experiment with other pairs of colours and see the effect.

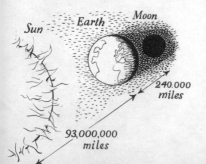

Sun
Earth
Moon
240,000 miles
93,000,000 miles

Making a Pinhole Camera

A pinhole camera works because light travels in straight lines.

To make a simple pinhole camera you need an empty tin, a piece of tissue (or greaseproof) paper and some thick brown paper. Cut out the closed end of the tin, and stick tissue paper over one open end and brown paper over the other. Make a pinhole in the middle of the brown paper—and there is your pinhole camera.

Hold it with the hole towards the window, cover your head and the tissue paper end of the tin with a dark cloth, and you should see a picture of the window. The picture you see will be upside down because the rays of light travelling in straight lines from the top and bottom of the window will have crossed as they pass through the pinhole. The diagram at the side shows how this happens.

To make a better pinhole camera you need two cardboard boxes which slide into each other. A box with a deep lid is ideal. Cut out a square from the bottom of the box and cover with brown paper. Then cut off the opposite end of the lid, and cover it completely with tissue paper. Make your pinhole in the brown paper as before.

You will again need to cover your head and the tissue paper end with a dark cloth. You can change the size of the picture by sliding one box into the other. The cloth over your head is necessary because very little light comes through the pinhole, and the picture is not very bright. See what happens if you make more than one pinhole, or if you make a large pinhole.

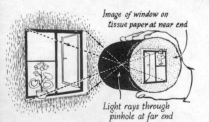

Image of window on tissue paper at near end

Light rays through pinhole at far end

Seeing Round Corners

Fix a small mirror upright in some plasticine on a piece of white paper. Darken the room and shine a torch through a comb so that you see rays of light on the white paper. See what happens when they strike the mirror. They are *reflected*. Turn the mirror slightly, and the direction of the reflected rays changes.

Because light can be reflected in this way you can hold a mirror round a doorway and see round the corner. That is how a periscope works. The commander of a submarine uses his periscope to see what is happening on the surface.

You can make a simple periscope with two small mirrors and a ruler. Fix the mirrors at the ends of the ruler with plasticine, setting them as in the picture. Put something on the table, as the boy has done.

Kneel down, holding the ruler upright with the top mirror over the edge of the table. Adjust the mirrors carefully until you see the object on the table in the bottom mirror. You have made a periscope.

The light from the teddy bear in the picture strikes

the top mirror, is reflected down into the lower one, and is again reflected into the boy's eyes. You can make a better periscope by using a cardboard tube with the mirrors firmly fixed inside, and with two square holes cut in the tube opposite them.

Images

The teddy bear the boy saw in the bottom mirror of his periscope is called the *image* of the teddy bear. The picture on the screen of the pinhole camera is an *image*. In a mirror you can see your own *image*.

If we use two mirrors we can get images of images. Hinge two small mirrors together with sticky tape, and stand them on the table as in the small diagram below. Place something—such as the toy Indian—in the angle between them.

Look into the mirrors and see how many images there are. Close up the mirrors slightly and see what happens to the number of images. As you continue to close the mirrors, watch how the number of images grows.

Unstick the mirrors and set them up, with dabs of plasticine, exactly facing each other, and put the Indian in the middle. Look over the top of one mirror into the other and you will see a line of Indians stretching away from you. These are *images* of *images* of the one Indian.

With two narrow mirrors of the same length you can make a toy called a *kaleidoscope*. Hinge them together down two long sides with sticky tape and join the open sides with cardboard. Paste some thin tissue paper over the bottom of this triangular tube. Put a few coloured beads and scraps of coloured paper down the tube.

Hold it over a light, look down the top and you will see a pattern like the one in the top corner of the picture, caused by reflections in the mirrors. When you shake the kaleidoscope you will get a new pattern.

14

Through the Looking–glass

Stand in front of a wardrobe mirror and look at the carpet. You will see exactly the same amount of carpet-pattern between the image of your feet and the mirror as there is between your feet and the mirror. This shows that your image is as far behind the mirror as you are in front of it. You can find where an image is by a simple experiment.

Put a sheet of white paper on the table, and set up a mirror in the middle with plasticine. Stand a tin soldier or something small about six inches in front of the mirror. Make sure that there is as much paper behind the mirror as in front.

Lay a ruler on the paper pointing towards the mirror. Kneel down, and looking along the edge of the ruler move it until it points straight at the image, just as if the ruler is a rifle you are aiming at the image of the soldier. When your aim is exactly right, hold the ruler firmly and draw a line along the edge right up to the mirror.

Aim at the soldier's image from several other points, until you have three or four lines ruled on the paper, all pointing to the mirror. Rule a line on the paper where the mirror is standing and draw a ring where the soldier is standing. Take away the mirror and the soldier.

Continue the lines with the ruler until they meet behind the line where the mirror was. This is the point where you saw the image of the soldier. Measure the distance from the mirror to the spot where the soldier stood, and to the spot where the image was. These distances should be the same.

16

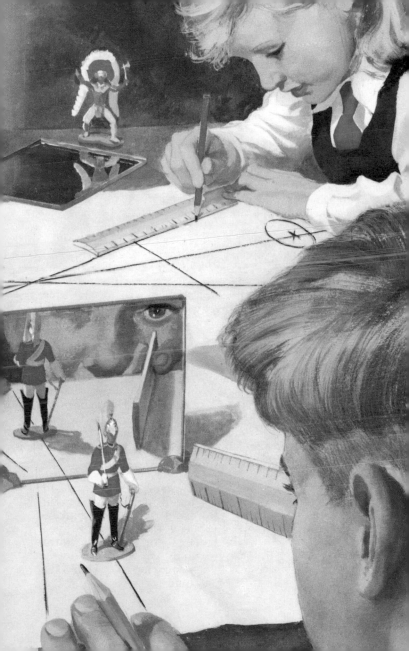

Pepper's Ghost

You do not have to use a mirror to see an image; you can see one in a plain sheet of glass. You will have seen your image in a shop window or in a glass-fronted book-case. This is the secret of a famous old stage trick, known as "Pepper's Ghost," invented a hundred years ago.

You can make a simple form of "Pepper's Ghost" yourself with a piece of glass, and mystify your friends by showing them a candle which seems to be alight in a glass of water.

You can see how it is done by looking at the picture and at the little diagram. The pile of books represents the side of a stage. The glass, which must be clean and polished, is set up on edge with two dabs of plasticine. The glass of water is moved about behind the glass until the candle appears to be alight inside it. You want a black book or a piece of black cloth for the background. Darken the room to get the best effect.

In the stage version of "Pepper's Ghost" an actor moves about at the side of the stage and out of sight, where you have the lighted candle. His image—the "ghost"—moves about the stage, seeming to walk through objects. The audience cannot see the glass from their seats, and the "ghost" is very real to them.

~ Plasticine

When "Pepper's Ghost" appears on the stage, the actor appears to be left-handed. Can you think out why that is? Move your hand in front of a mirror and see which hand your image moves. Think that out!

18

Bending Light

We have found out how the direction of a ray of light is altered when it strikes a mirror or a polished surface. Rays of light also bend in another way.

Soak an empty medicine bottle so that the label comes off, and fill it with water. Add four drops of milk, put the cork back, and shake the bottle. Put a sheet of white paper on the table and lay the medicine bottle on its wide side. Cut a slit in a piece of card and hold it over the front of a torch, so that only a thin ray of light shines. Darken the room and hold the torch so that the ray of light strikes the side of the medicine bottle. Look carefully at the ray of light. You will see that it bends; it changes its direction as it goes into the water.

This is the secret of the disappearing coin trick. Put a penny in the bottom of an empty bowl and stand it on the table. Look at the penny along the edge of a ruler, and when you can see it, lower your hand a little so that you can just *not* see the coin. Keep quite still while someone pours water into the bowl. Gradually the penny will come into view. The light coming from the penny to your eye is bent.

Rays of light coming from things under the water

bend when they pass through the surface. This makes swimming pools and clear rivers seem to be shallower than they really are. A pencil standing half in water seems to be bent; try it and see.

Lenses

Fill a jam-jar with water, add two or three drops of milk, and stand it on a sheet of white paper. Produce rays of light from a torch shining through two slits in a card and see what happens when they pass through the jam-jar. They bend, and come to a point on the far side. The jam-jar full of water is a "water lens," which makes the rays of light come together, or *converge*. Rays of light bend in the same way when they pass through glass.

Glass lenses are used in many different ways in every-day life. There are lenses in spectacles, cameras, magnifying glasses, telescopes, microscopes, binoculars—see if you can think of some more.

There are two kinds of lens. A lens which is thicker in the middle than at the edge is a *convex lens*, like your jam-jar or a simple magnifying glass. A lens which is thicker at the edge than in the middle is a *concave lens*.

You will need lenses for the next few experiments. Perhaps you have a magnifying glass or old-fashioned circular spectacle lenses which your parents might be able to find. Ask them to take the lenses out of the frames. You may have a torch with a useful lens in it.

Side view of Lenses

Convex   *Concave*

22

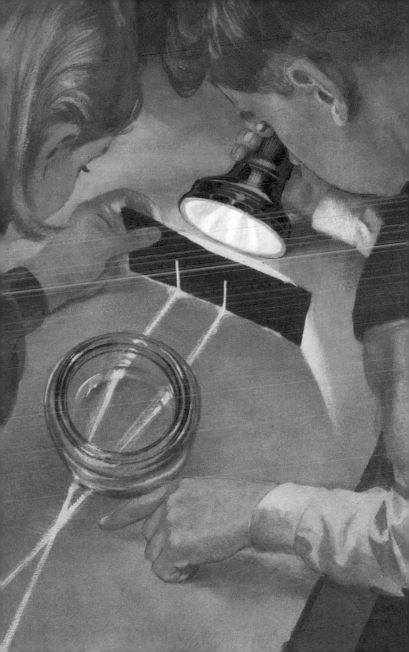

Burning Glasses and Spectacles

The sun's rays can be brought to a point or "focus" by a convex lens to produce a very bright spot of light which is, in fact, an image of the sun. The heat rays from the sun are also brought to the same focus. With a convex lens you can concentrate enough heat in one spot, on a bright summer day, to scorch a piece of paper. You can even light a camp fire, which is why a convex lens is sometimes called a "burning glass."

A goldfish bowl is a convex lens, as we found out on page 6, and it could set a house on fire. If the bowl is on a window-sill in direct sunlight in summer, and the focus happens to fall on a curtain, it could set it alight. But all goldfish keepers know that goldfish should never be left in bright sunlight.

A common use for lenses is, of course, for spectacles. Your eyes contain a special lens (see diagram, page 6) which helps to form the image on the retina. Sometimes, for various reasons, the image does not fall exactly on the retina of the eye, and then a person does not see clearly. An optician tests and examines that person's eyes to find out what kind of lenses are needed to correct his vision. These lenses are fitted into frames to make a pair of spectacles.

Nearly every pair of spectacles is different, and often the two lenses in one pair differ. Some spectacles have two lenses in one, so that they can be used for seeing long distances and for reading; these are called "bi-focal" lenses. Lens-making is a highly skilled craft.

24

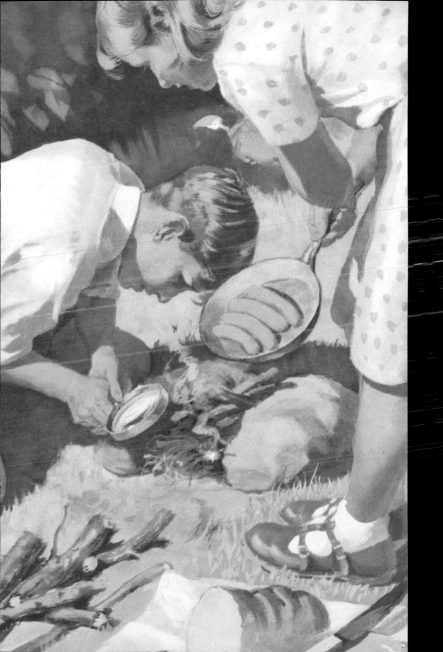

Fat Lenses and Thin Lenses

We shall only be using *convex* lenses in our experiments in this book, lenses which are thicker in the middle than at the edge. Some convex lenses are very thick, and others are slender. If we are to use lenses we must know one particular thing about them—their *focal length*.

Fix a convex lens upright with plasticine on the "O" mark on a ruler. Aim at the window or an electric light in the far corner of the room, as in the diagram. Hold a piece of white paper upright on the ruler and move it backwards and forwards until you can see a sharp image of the window or the light. Read off the measurement on the ruler exactly where the card is.

The distance from the lens to the paper is the *focal length* of that lens. Chubby lenses have a short focal length, thin ones have a longer focal length. Find the focal length of any other lenses you have. Note each measurement on a small piece of paper, and stick it to the edge of each lens.

When you know the focal length of a lens you can make a simple projector to throw a picture on the wall. Cover the front of a torch with tissue paper, and fix a piece of cinema film over it—upside down—with sticky paper and so that light only passes through the film. Darken the room and hold your lens in front of the torch at about one-and-a-half times the focal length.

Image of
window
on paper

Lens

Focal length

When the lens is at the right distance, you will get an enlarged image of the film on the wall. You will find that the picture will be upside down if the piece of film is the right way up, so film is always put in a projector upside down.

Making a Toy Camera

The first step in making a toy camera is to find the focal length of your lens. Set it at the end of a ruler, as you did in the previous experiment, put a lighted candle on the table and hold the lens about four feet away from it. Move a card up and down the ruler until you see a small image of the candle.

The distance from the card to the lens will give you, roughly, its focal length. You will probably be able to use the pin-hole box camera you made on page 10, provided the two parts slide apart to the focal length of the lens.

The two parts of the cardboard box which slide together must fit so that no light can leak through. You can use two fitting cardboard tubes instead. Cut off the bottom of one of the boxes or tubes and cover it with tissue paper, fixed with sticky paper round the edge. Cut a hole in the opposite end, about half an inch across. Fix the lens here with a ring of plasticine or sticky tape. Focus the camera by sliding the boxes in or out until you get a clear image on the tissue paper. The image, of course, will be upside down.

In a real camera the film goes where you have tissue paper. It is covered with a chemical substance which is affected by light. The shutter over the lens is only open long enough to let in just sufficient light to affect the chemical on the film, and make the image permanent. This film, with the image on it, becomes the *negative*.

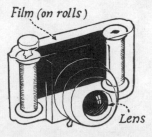

Film (on rolls)

Lens

28

Making a Microscope

You have seen that a convex lens can throw a large image on the wall, or a small image on the film of a camera. It can also be used as a simple magnifying glass. Hold it very close to the object you want to examine and not too close to your eye, and move the lens towards your eye until you see the object very much enlarged. A magnifying glass like this is useful for looking at foreign stamps, small pond creatures, insects and most small things of interest.

For looking at very small things you need a *microscope*, which has two lenses and magnifies in two steps. The lens nearest the object forms a magnified image, which is magnified again by the other lens.

If you have two convex lenses, you can make a microscope. One lens should have a short focal length, about two or three inches. The focal length of the other should be longer, say four or five inches. Set the lenses up on a ruler with plasticine, so that their distance apart is equal to *twice* the focal length of the thick lens, *added* to the focal length of the thin lens. For example, if the thick lens has a focal length of 2 inches, and the thin one 4 inches, set them up $2 \times 2 + 4$ inches, which is 8 inches apart.

Look through your microscope at some small object, with the thin lens nearest to your eye. You may need to adjust the position of the lenses slightly. A real microscope enables you to see objects invisible to the naked eye, and magnified up to about *three hundred times*.

30

Making a Telescope

A microscope is used for examining objects close to you. A telescope is used to look at far-away things. When a sailor uses his telescope he sees things the right way up, but the astronomer, looking at the stars, sees them upside down, because his telescope is slightly different. The telescope you can make will be like the astronomer's, with the images upside down.

You need the same two lenses you used to make the microscope, one with a short focal length, the other longer. You simply add the focal lengths together and fix the lenses on the ruler that distance apart. This time look through the *thicker lens*, so you put that one at the end of the ruler nearest to you. Look at a distant object and adjust the further lens slightly to suit your own eyes.

The invention of the microscope and telescope, more than three hundred years ago, led to discoveries of immense importance. With their powerful microscopes,

doctors were able to see the very tiny organisms which cause disease, and discover how to fight them. Scientists use the microscope for their research. The powerful modern telescope enables the astronomer to see further and further out into space.

32

Curved Mirrors

We have found out some of the things we can do with flat mirrors; now let us find out about curved mirrors. A polished spoon is the simplest form of curved mirror. The inside is a *concave* reflector, the back a *convex* reflector. Look at your own reflection in the inside of a large polished spoon, moving it up to, and then away from, your face. Then do the same with the back of the spoon. What do you notice?

When you look into the inside of the spoon your face appears large when it is close, and small and upside down when you hold it away from you. Looking into the back your face always seems to be small and the right way up. Sometimes there is a convex mirror on the sitting room wall, in which you can see all the room. A car driving mirror may be the same kind, to show the driver as much of the road behind him as possible.

If your father has a concave shaving mirror ask him to lend it to you. Put it in the sun and hold a piece of white card in front of it—where the rays are brought together into a small bright spot. The distance from the card to the middle of the mirror is its focal length.

Now stand the mirror on a table in a darkened room and put a lighted candle at the focus. Move it about until you get a bright spot on the wall. You have made a model searchlight. A real searchlight, a car headlamp, or a torch has the light at the focus of a concave reflector to throw a narrow beam of light. At the fair it is the large concave and convex mirrors which give you those amusing distorted reflections.

Looking at the Moon

A concave mirror, instead of a lens, was used by Sir Isaac Newton three hundred years ago to make the first *reflecting* telescope. Ever since astronomers have used reflecting telescopes to look at the stars. The largest in the world, at Mount Palomar, in America, has a reflecting mirror 200 inches across, that is sixteen feet eight inches. Newton's was only about four inches across. The famous radio telescope at Jodrell Bank, in England, has an enormous concave "dish" which reflects radio waves instead of light waves.

You can make a simple reflecting telescope with a concave shaving mirror, a lens and a small flat mirror. Choose a clear moonlit night and take your apparatus outside. Stand the shaving mirror on a window-sill or on a garden table, pointing to the moon.

Hold the small flat mirror so that you can see in it an image of the shaving mirror, with the moon in the middle. Now look at that reflection with your magnifying glass, and you will see a magnified image of the moon. That is how a reflecting telescope works.

If you can borrow a good pair of binoculars you can study the moon. The best time is at half-moon, when you can see the craters and the so-called "seas" on the moon's surface, 240,000 miles away.

36

The Moon

What is moonlight? It is *not* light produced by the moon! Moonlight is light from the sun, which strikes the moon and is scattered or reflected. Part of this reflected light reaches us on the earth, and that is what we call moonlight.

The shape of the moon *appears* to change, because it moves round the earth. You can find out how this happens by an experiment with a torch and a tennis ball.

Stand in a darkened room with your back to a torch, arranged so that it shines over your head. Hold a tennis ball *in front of you and higher than your head*, to be in the light of the torch. The torch is the sun, your head is the earth, and the ball is the moon.

You will see the half of the ball facing you completely lighted up. This is *Full Moon*. Make a quarter turn, like the girl in the picture, so that you are standing sideways to the torch. You will now only see half a side of the ball lighted up; that is *Half Moon*. Now turn through another quarter so that you are facing the torch. The

side of the ball you see is in darkness; that is when no moon is seen from the earth.

A complete turn round with the ball will show you all the changes (or *phases*) of the moon which occur in a little more than four weeks, which we call a *lunar month*.

38

The Stars

All daylight comes from the sun, which is 93,000,000 (ninety-three million) miles away. Think of that for a moment; think of one mile, then a hundred miles, then a thousand miles, then a *thousand* thousand miles, and finally ninety-three times that! Light travels this enormous distance in about eight minutes, at the incredible speed of 186,000 miles a *second*.

The sun is a star, and is the nearest one to us. The next nearest very bright star is Alpha Centauri. The light from this star takes four-and-a-half years to reach us, even though light travels at 186,000 miles a *second*. Think of that for a few moments.

Stars are so immensely far away that astronomers do not measure distances in miles, but in *light years*. A light year is the distance light travels in a year. That is something else to think about!

The stars we see, some of which are *millions* of light years away, form unchanging patterns, and some of these patterns, called *constellations* have names. It is a help in recognising constellations if you make a "constellation viewer". Get a star chart, or a picture of the constellations in a book, and trace one on thin paper. Put the paper on a postcard and prick the stars through the card. Mark each pinprick with a cross and write the name of the constellation on the card.

On a starlit night hold your card over a torch and the card will show the constellation as spots of light. With this you can find the real constellation in the sky.

40

Pole Star

Big Dipper

Light and Colour

The geologist finds out what the earth is made of by chipping off pieces of rock and examining them in his laboratory. The astronomer, who studies the stars, is not so fortunate. He cannot chip pieces off a star, he has nothing to work on but the light which comes from it.

Because light from a star is very faint the astronomer has to collect as much as he possibly can, and so the huge reflecting telescopes are built. The light collected in the 200-inch reflecting dish is passed through a special instrument called a *spectrograph*. This splits up the light from a star into various colours, called its *spectrum*, and and by studying this spectrum the astronomer can find what substances the star is made of.

You can split the sun's light into its colours quite simply. Put about an inch of water in a flat dish and lean a small handbag mirror at one end. Arrange the dish so that sunlight falls on the surface of the water. The light will go through the water and will be reflected by the mirror. The light that comes out will be split and will show bands of colour on the ceiling, the wall or a sheet of paper. This is a *spectrum*.

A spectrum is also formed when sunlight falls on cut glass, raindrops and on the edges of mirrors. The spectrum formed with raindrops is, of course, the rainbow.

The Spectrum

In the experiment on the previous page you made a band of colour from sunlight. The colours came from the "white" light of the sun, and in their proper order the colours of the *spectrum* are:—red, orange, yellow, green, blue, indigo and violet. You noticed that the colours merged gradually from one to another.

This breaking up of white light into the colours of the spectrum was discovered by Sir Isaac Newton, who realised that the white light is really a mixture of colours. He also discovered that if the colours of the spectrum were mixed, he got white light once more. You can prove this by making what is called "Newton's disc."

Cut a circle of cardboard about six inches across and divide it into seven sections. Paint these sections with the colours of the spectrum, as above, and in that order. Mount the card on a cotton reel and put a pencil through

the hole and through the card. This is a top; spin it fast and you will see the colours merge together and the card seems to be white. In fact it will probably be grey, because the colours from your paintbox are not the pure colours of the spectrum.

What Colour is it?

Why does a leaf look green, or a red motor bus look red? You might think that a silly question, but a scientist often has to ask questions which seem obvious. Shine a torch on to a red book, and hold a piece of white paper so that the light from the book is reflected on to it. The white paper is tinted red. It is no longer white paper. Why?

Although all the colours of the spectrum were in the white light from the torch, only the red was reflected from the book. The other colours were absorbed by the red colouring of the book. In the same way a green leaf appears green because it absorbs all colours except green, which it reflects.

Here is an interesting experiment with colour. Draw an elephant like the one in the picture. Paint a *green* howdah and mahout on the elephant's back, but do *not* outline it. Now paint the rest of the elephant red.

Cover the end of a torch with green transparent wrapping, darken the room and shine the green light on your picture.

You will see the elephant clearly, but the howdah and mahout will almost disappear. The reason is that the white background and the green howdah reflect the green light, so they merge together. Try it with red transparent paper over the torch.

Optical Illusions

Have you ever made flicker pictures? A dozen pieces of thin card, or an old note-book is all you need. Draw a pin-man with his arms by his sides. Draw him again, pricking the paper to mark the position of his head and feet, for he must be in exactly the same place and the same size. This time move his arms up a little. Keep on drawing him with his arms moving up a little more each time and then down again. When you flick the pages through the figure will come to life.

How does this happen? On page 24 we found out about images being formed on the retina of the eye. These images do not disappear immediately, they last for a fraction of a second. When you flick the pages the images overlap, and the motion of the pin-man seems to be continuous. At the cinema about twenty-five different pictures are shown every second, so we see a continuous movement.

An interesting optical illusion is the "canary in the cage." Get a piece of white card about two inches square.

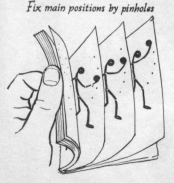

Fix main positions by pinholes

On one side draw a bird cage, on the other a canary. Fit this card into a slot made in a short piece of stick, preferably round. Roll the stick backwards and forwards between the palms of your hands as fast as you can. The canary will appear to be inside his cage.

Light and Life

Light is essential to life. You can show by an experiment what happens to a living thing when it is deprived of light. Ask to be allowed to experiment with a plant in the garden, or with a pot plant, preferably one with broad leaves, such as a geranium. Cover a leaf on both sides with black paper. Cover another with clear cellophane.

Leave them for a week and then take off both coverings. You should find that the leaf which was covered by the black envelope is pale and unhealthy looking, while the other is normal. You may wonder why you had to cover a leaf with clear cellophane. That is what is called a *control* in the experiment; it made sure that it was the absence of light which affected the leaf and not the fact that it was covered.

It is the light absorbed by the leaves of a plant which cause the changes which must take place it if is to grow. If there is no light the plant will not develop. All plants struggle for light, and in a forest there is little growth on the ground. In the dark jungle the trees grow tall in their efforts to reach the light. Flowers on a window-sill turn to the light.

You feel better when the sun shines after dull days. We need light and warmth just as plants do, and without light we are pale and sickly. In fact light is so vital that without it there would be no life at all.

Here is a list of the few articles you will need for the experiments in this book. You will probably have most of them.

An electric torch.
Small mirrors.
Magnifying glass.
Old spectacle lenses
                 (convex type).
A shaving mirror.
A piece of glass
                 (about 12″ x 12″).
A candle.
Coloured and clear cellophane.
A glass tumbler.